PRESERVED STEAM ON THE WEST HIGHLAND RAILWAY

DAVID PRICE

AMBERLEY

Front cover: Class 5 No. 44871 on Glenfinnan viaduct with the Jacobite to Mallaig on 10 October 2016.

Back cover: LNER-liveried K4 No. 3442 *The Great Marquess* and K1 No. 2005 leave Glenfinnan with the return working to Fort William on 10 August 1994.

First published 2024

Amberley Publishing
The Hill, Stroud
Gloucestershire, GL5 4EP

www.amberley-books.com

ISBN 978 1 3981 1970 3 (print)
ISBN 978 1 3981 1971 0 (ebook)

British Library Cataloguing in Publication Data.
A catalogue record for this book is available from the British Library.

Typesetting by SJmagic DESIGN SERVICES, India.
Printed in the UK.

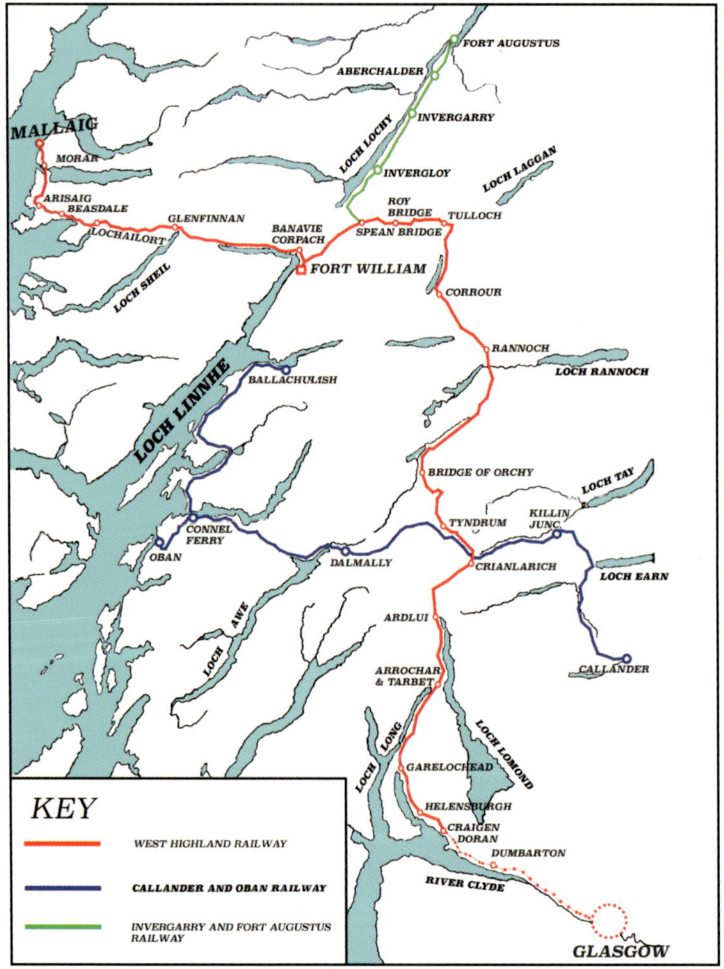

Railways in the West Highlands. (Drawn by Conor Phillimore-Price)

INTRODUCTION

Apart from a narrowing strip along the northern bank of the River Clyde, the region to the north-west of Glasgow is a land of mountains, deep valleys and long lochs. A railway to Helensburgh was opened in 1858, but beyond there it was sparsely populated with few towns and no industry. Further north in central Scotland, a line had been opened to Callander and in 1857 an Act was passed to build an east–west route onwards to Oban on the west coast. However, despite backing from the Caledonian Railway, the Callander & Oban had continuing financial problems. Progress was slow and it took to August 1873 to reach Tyndrum, less than halfway. It finally reached Oban in June 1880.

Glasgow now had a railway to the west coast, but it involved a time-consuming and circuitous route via Stirling, so thoughts turned to a more direct route northwards. This led to the formation of the Glasgow & North Western Railway which proposed a line from Glasgow along the eastern side of Loch Lomond to Crianlarich, skirting Rannoch Moor, through Glencoe, on to Fort William and continuing through the Great Glen to Inverness. A bill was presented to Parliament in November 1882 with the line to be worked by the North British Railway. However, there was major opposition from rival companies, landowners and the Caledonian Canal Commission, which led to the bill being defeated and plans being withdrawn on 31 May 1883.

Following the findings of the Crofters Commission Report, there was sympathy for the plight of the population in the Western Highlands and in 1889 a new company, the West Highland Railway, backed by the North British, proposed a different route to Fort William. This left the Helensburgh line at Craigendoran, passing Gare Loch, along the western side of Loch Lomond and through Glenfalloch to Crianlarich, where it would cross the Oban line. Having reached Bridge of Orchy via Strathfillan, it headed due north across Rannoch Moor before dropping down to Glen Spean and approaching Fort William from the north-east. From there it was planned to extend westwards to Roshven on the west coast.

There was again opposition from rival companies, but the route to Fort William had been carefully chosen so that it mainly passed through the estates of major landowners who would not oppose the scheme. It was a different story west of Fort William where strong opposition forced the abandonment of the extension. The bill was approved in Parliament on 3 July 1889 and building started in October, although progress was slow with a dispute between the company and their contractors and difficulties in establishing a permanent way across the boggy Rannoch Moor. The line finally opened on 7 August 1894, with a short branch to Banavie on the Caledonian Canal added in June 1895.

One of the reasons for establishing the railway had been to tap into the lucrative fish traffic from the west coast, so another attempt to extend was made. Mallaig was chosen as the terminus. This time landowners were more cooperative and the West Highland Railway (Mallaig Extension) Bill was passed. There was a government grant for the scheme, which also involved the building of a harbour at Mallaig, although some parliamentary opposition to this delayed progress until an Amended Act was passed in August 1896.

Construction started in 1897 with Robert McAlpine and Sons as contractors. They were among the pioneers of the use of concrete and this was used for the building of the bridges and viaducts on the line, including the spectacular curving Glenfinnan structure, now well known for its association with the Harry Potter films. The extension started from a point on the Banavie branch, in effect shortening that to less than a mile and finished at Mallaig, 42 miles from Fort William. It was officially opened on 1 April 1901, worked by the North British, which eventually took over the West Highland in December 1908.

There were further attempts to build a line through the Great Glen to Inverness but with the Highland Railway determined to keep rival companies out of Inverness they all failed. Eventually a small private company, the Invergarry & Fort Augustus Railway, won approval to build a line from Spean Bridge to the southern end of Loch Ness. Beset by financial difficulties, it finally opened in July 1903, but it generated very little traffic and was a colossal waste of money. The other railway development in the West Highlands was the opening of a line from Connel Ferry, near Oban, north to Ballachullish in 1903. Proposals to extend the 12 miles to Fort William came to nothing.

The North British continued to operate the West Highland until the Grouping in 1923 when it became part of the London & North Eastern Railway. The Banavie branch closed in September 1939, with passenger services to Fort Augustus ceasing in 1933, although there was minimal freight traffic until 1946. Following nationalisation of the railways in 1948, a Scottish Region was established, so ex-London Midland & Scottish engines and BR Standard classes joined the LNER engines on the line until diesels took over in the 1960s. The future of the whole line became an area of great concern during the railway closures threatened by the Beeching Report, but the establishment of the large Scottish Pulp Factory at Corpach with the associated extra freight traffic helped to avert closure. The section of line from Dunblane to Crianlarich on the original Callander and Oban route did close in 1965, so traffic for Oban now goes north from Glasgow and uses the link between the lines at Crianlarich. The Ballachullish branch closed in March 1966.

In an attempt to generate more usage of the Mallaig line, ScotRail introduced steam excursions on the extension in May 1984. The privately owned engines were towed to Fort William, but in 1987 they were allowed to work south on specials organised by the Scottish Railway Preservation Society. InterCity special trains took over the Mallaig Steam Service in the 1990s, but with privatisation of the railways looming they decided to pull out after 1994.

West Coast Railways started to operate the service in 1995, renaming it the Jacobite, and it has grown to be very successful with trains running seven days a week for some six months of the year. The stock is sometimes steam-hauled from Craigendoran Junction to Fort William and vice versa at the start and end of the operating season and there are occasional other steam excursions from and to Glasgow.

Since preserved steam returned to the West Highland in 1984 some fifteen different engines have been seen at Fort William and pictures of them all appear in this volume. Thanks are due to the organisers of the various photographic charters that have been arranged over the years. These give enthusiasts the opportunity of recording runpasts in otherwise inaccessible parts of the line. Although there is a turntable at Fort William, there are no facilities to turn engines at Mallaig, so there is tender first running in one direction on the extension. The engines usually run chimney first from Fort William, so it is always interesting to see one facing east.

Trains to and from Fort William use part of the electrified line to Helensburgh Central and here Nos 45407 and 62005 pass Cardross with a stock move on 12 October 2009.

LNER-liveried K4 No. 3442 and K1 No. 2005 leave Craigendoran Junction with the West Highland Centenary Tour on 7 August 1994.

Class 5 No. 45231 and K1 No. 62005 approach Helensburgh Upper with the Jacobite stock to Fort William on 14 May 2009.

Class 5s Nos 45407 and 44871 at Faslane with empty stock to Carnforth on 30 October 2010.

Nos 45407 and 62005 leave Arrochar and Tarbet station with the Jacobite stock returning to Carnforth on 12 October 2009.

Nos 45407 and 44871 head south near Pulpit Rock on 30 October 2010. Loch Lomond is just visible to the right.

Class 5 No. 45407 leaves Ardlui with a tour to Mallaig on 3 September 2005.

K1 No. 2005 and Class 5 No. 44767 cross the viaduct in Glenfalloch with a southbound tour on a misty 22 October 1994.

No. 62005 crosses the viaduct in Glenfalloch with the Great Britain X leg to Fort William on 3 May 2017.

B1 No. 1264 in LNER livery at Derrydaroch with a tour from Oban to Glasgow on 3 October 1999.

Nos 3442 and 2005 at Derrydaroch with the Centenary Special on 7 August 1994.

Now in BR livery as No. 61994, K4 *The Great Marquess* heads south from Crianlarich with the West Highlander Tour on 2 September 2007.

B1 No. 61306 crosses the A85 as it approaches Crianlarich with the Highlands and Islands Tour from Fort William on 15 May 2019.

In the guise of long-scrapped classmates, the K1 and B1 No. 61264 cross the River Fillan during the West Highland charter on 5 October 2002.

No. 45231 leads No. 62005 over the foot crossing at Inverhaggernie with a northbound stock move on 14 May 2009.

B1 No. 61306 passes Inverhaggernie with the Steam Dreams Tour to Fort William on 13 May 2019.

A little later, No. 61306 climbs away from Tyndrum on 13 May 2019.

K1 No. 62005, running as No. 62012, and B1 No. 61264, running as No. 61243, approach County March Summit during the charter of 5 October 2002.

In LMS livery, Class 5 No. 5407 climbs to County March Summit with the Scottish Railway Preservation Society (SRPS) tour from Fort William on 24 October 1992.

K4 No. 61994 rounds the Horseshoe Curve with the West Highlander to Oban on 5 September 2010.

Nos 45407 and 62005 cross Allt Coralan viaduct in the Horseshoe with empty stock on 12 October 2009.

K1 No. 2005 crosses Allt Kinglass viaduct with the SRPS tour from Fort William on 14 November 1987.

Nos 45407 and 62005 approach the Horseshoe Curve with a stock move to Carnforth on 12 October 2009.

Viewed from the overbridge on the West Highland Way, autumn colours abound as a pair of Class 5s head south from Bridge of Orchy on 30 October 2010.

Class 5 No. 5407 leaves Bridge of Orchy with the Claymore Tour from Fort William on 24 October 1992.

Nos 45231 and 62005 leave Bridge of Orchy with the Jacobite stock from Carnforth on 14 May 2009.

B1 No. 61306 north of Bridge of Orchy with the Steam Dreams Tour to Fort William on 13 May 2019.

High above Loch Tulla, No. 62005 works north with the Great Britain X leg on 3 May 2017.

On the route it was designed for, No. 61994 *The Great Marquess* works north past Loch Tulla with the West Highlander of 4 September 2010.

Nos 3442 and 2005 pass Achallader with the Centenary Special on 7 August 1994.

Running as classmate No. 62012, K1 No. 62005 nears Gorton with a runpast for the charter participants on 6 October 2002.

No. 62005 crosses Garbh Ghaoir viaduct south of Rannoch during the charter of 6 October 2002.

B1 No. 61264 leaves the remote station of Rannoch with empty stock to Fort William on 25 May 2006.

No. 45407 runs light engine across Rannoch viaduct on 11 October 2008.

With Loch Eigheach in the background, No. 61264 crosses Rannoch viaduct on 25 May 2006.

Standard Class 4 No. 76079, renumbered as No. 76001, north of Rannoch station on 11 October 2008.

No. 76079 as 76001 passes Lochan A Chlaidheimh, also known as the Loch of the Sword, during the charter on 11 October 2008.

The Standard 4 on Rannoch Moor on 11 October 2008.The West Highland charters were a great way to reach otherwise inaccessible locations.

The embankment north of Corrour station is the setting for No. 45407 on 11 October 2008.

The splendid LNER combination of K1 and B1 run out of the shadows near Corrour during the charter on 6 October 2002.

An earlier runpast on 6 October 2002 with Nos 61264 and 62005 climbing away from Loch Treig and onto Rannoch Moor.

Class 5 No. 45407 leaves Tulloch with the Railway Touring Company's West Highlander Tour to Glasgow on 21 September 2014.

K1 No. 2005 approaches the Fersit road bridge with the southbound SRPS tour of 14 November 1987.

Double-headed Class 5s near Murlaggan with the SRPS tour to Polmont on 27 October 2012.

With the first southbound steam tour from Fort William on 17 October 1987, Class 5 No. 5305 has just passed Cille Choirill, a fifteenth-century chapel up on the hillside.

Class 5 No. 5407 takes the curve away from the Monessie Gorge with the Claymore Tour on 24 October 1992.

Class 5 No. 5305 hauls InterCity stock away from Monessie on 23 October 1989. It worked as far as Crianlarich before returning light engine to Fort William.

A view into Monessie Gorge as B1 No. 61306 takes the Steam Dreams Tour south on 15 May 2019.

K4 No. 61994 near Achnabobane with the southbound West Highlander on 2 September 2007.

Seen from the edge of Fort William golf course, K1 No. 2005 heads south with the SRPS train on 14 November 1987.

With black skies all around, a welcome burst of sun highlights B1 No. 61264 and Standard Class 4 No. 75014 leaving Fort William on 23 September 2000.

Class 5 No. 44871 works south from Fort William with the SRPS tour of 16 October 1993.

Fort William station on 23 May 2004 with Standard Class 4 No. 76079 running round the stock of a private charter. It was running as No. 76001, a former Fort William engine.

Class 5 No. 45212 works past Fort William yard with the Jacobite to Mallaig on 15 May 2019.

Seen from the footbridge at the northern end of the yard, K1 No. 62005 heads west on 26 October 2012.

North British 0-6-0 No. 673 *Maude* passes the depot with a special on 28 May 1984. The veteran engine caused several fires on the way west.

K4 No. 3442 *The Great Marquess* on shed at Fort William on 16 July 1989.

No. 5972 *Olton Hall*, used as *Hogwarts Castle* in the Harry Potter films, in Fort William depot on 24 September 2001. Filming took place around Glenfinnan.

K1 No. 62005 crosses the Lochy viaduct on the way to Mallaig on 6 June 2013.

Standard Class No. 75014 on the Lochy viaduct on 21 September 2000.

Class 5 No. 44871 crosses the Lochy River with the afternoon service to Mallaig on 4 June 2013. The remains of Inverlochy Castle can be seen above the engine.

During the first weekend of the West Highlander service, No. 5407 approaches the level crossing at Banavie on 27 May 1984.

With Ben Nevis as backdrop, Class 5 No. 44932 nears Banavie on 30 August 1986.

No. 5305 has just crossed the Caledonian Canal with the luxury Queen of Scots train on 19 October 1990. The new signalling centre can be seen beyond the bridge.

The view from the jetty at Corpach as B1 No. 61264 heads west on 24 September 2002.

Class 5 No. 44871 heads away from Corpach on 10 October 2016. A marina has since been built here.

Standard Class 4 No. 75014 at Fassfern with the Jacobite of 23 September 1998.

No. 44871 is reflected in the waters of Loch Eil at Fassfern on 11 October 2013.

No. 5407 passes Corribeg with the Royal Scotsman leg on 9 October 1991. This luxury touring train still operates on the line with diesel haulage.

No. 5305 near Kinlocheil with the Queen of Scots train to Mallaig on 9 November 1990.

On a day with exceptional visibility, No. 44871 crosses the wetlands beyond Loch Eil with the afternoon Jacobite on 7 June 2013.

Specially turned to face east for the charter, No. 62005 approaches the wetlands overbridge on the return to Fort William on 9 October 2004.

Forestry clearance opened up this view as No. 62005 nears Glenfinnan on the way to Mallaig on 18 September 2020.

No. 75014 nears the bridge over the A830 on the approach to Glenfinnan on 7 September 1995.

There are spectacular autumn colours around as No. 62005 is seen near Craigag Lodge on 26 October 2012.

With the green-and-cream rake then in use, K4 No. 3442 *The Great Marquess* has just left the tunnel near Craigag Lodge on the way west on 16 July 1989.

The rare sight of a double-header on the extension as the K4 and K1 cross Glenfinnan viaduct with the return to Fort William on 10 August 1994.

The curved construction of the Glenfinnan viaduct is clearly seen as No. 44871 crosses on 12 October 2013.

Mist was just clearing as No. 62005 climbs away from the viaduct with the service to Mallaig on 24 October 2012.

North British No. 673 *Maude* works hard up Glenfinnan Bank with the special on 28 May 1984. Despite the destination board, the train only got as far as Arisaig.

Unusually facing east, B1 No. 61264 leaves Glenfinnan station with the Jacobite returning to Fort William on 24 September 2001.

No. 44871 climbs away from Glenfinnan with the westbound train on 10 October 2016.

Carrying an unusual headboard, Class 5 No. 44767 rounds the curves away from Glenfinnan on 18 September 1997.

The K1 runs alongside the stream west of Glenfinnan on 26 October 2012.

In superb autumnal conditions, No. 62005 leaves a long steam trail back towards Glenfinnan on 24 October 2012.

No. 44871 approaches the overbridge west of Glenfinnan with the Royal Scotsman to Mallaig on 6 September 1989.

No. 62005 near Glenfinnan Summit on 5 June 2013.

Running as No. 76001, Standard Class 4 No. 76079 rounds the curve high above Loch Eilt during the charter on 12 October 2008.

Renumbered as No. 62011, K1 No. 62005 works eastbound round Loch Eilt on 30 September 2007.

The view across Loch Eilt as the veteran 0-6-0 *Maude* returns tender first from Arisaig on 28 May 1984.

Once again renumbered for the charter, this time as No. 62012, the K1 crosses the causeway at the western end of Loch Eilt on 9 October 2004.

8F No. 48151 worked several seasons on the Jacobite and is seen here crossing the Loch Eilt causeway on the way to Mallaig on 20 September 1995.

Class 5 No. 45212 rounds the edge of Loch Eilt with the afternoon working to Mallaig on 11 May 2021.

No. 44871 passes the rockface at Lochailort on the way west on 7 June 2013.

No. 62005 heads away from Lochailort on 7 June 2013.

8F No. 48151 on the embankment between Lochailort and Polnish on 19 September 1995.

No. 44871 nears Polnish on 11 October 2013.

LNER-liveried K4 No. 3442 *The Great Marquess* heads west at Polnish on 16 July 1989.

No. 62005 passes Polnish on the way west on the crisp autumn morning of 24 October 2012.

During the period it ran in LNER livery, K1 No. 2005 passes Our Lady of the Braes Chapel with the Royal Scotsman on 2 September 1987.

Now in BR livery and running as classmate No. 62012, the K1 passes Loch Dubh on the way back to Fort William on 9 October 2004.

No. 62005 crosses the rarely photographed Arnabol viaduct on 13 May 2021.

During the period it faced east, B1 No. 61264 crosses Loch Nan Uamh viaduct on the way back to Fort William on 4 September 2001.

No. 62005 on Loch Nan Uamh viaduct with the West Highlander Tour to Mallaig on 21 September 2014.

The view down Loch Nan Uamh as No. 45212 crosses the viaduct with the afternoon train on 17 September 2020.

No. 44871 climbs Beasdale Bank on the afternoon of 6 June 2013.

No. 62005 nears Beasdale Summit on 26 October 2012.

Standard Class 4 No. 75014 on the curve at Borrodale on 5 September 1996.

No. 44871 in Borrodale on 5 June 2013. The overbridge has weight restriction signs but vehicle access is virtually impossible.

No. 45212 approaches Arisaig station on 14 May 2019.

In LMS livery, Class 5 No. 5305 glints nicely as it leaves Arisaig with the Queen of Scots train on 9 November 1990.

Seen from the other side of the line, No. 62005 heads away from Arisaig with the West Highlander Tour of 21 September 2014.

With no way of turning engines at Mallaig, tender-first running is necessary one way as the renumbered K1 and B1 approach Arisaig heading back to Fort William on 7 October 2003.

No. 45407 at Kinloid with the Jacobite to Fort William on 12 October 2016.

K4 No. 3442 and K1 No. 2005 climb Kinloid Bank on the way east on 10 August 1994.

No. 75014 passes the small ruin at Kinloid on 20 September 2000. The distinctive shapes of the Small Isles can be seen in the background.

Looking across the Silver Sands, No. 45212 nears Morar on 11 May 2021.

No. 62005 on Morar viaduct with the morning Jacobite on 10 May 2021.

Loch Morar is just visible in the background as No. 45212 leaves Morar on 17 September 2020.

No. 62005 is nearing the end of its journey as it nears Mallaig on 18 September 2020.

No. 45407 makes a vigorous departure from Mallaig with the return to Fort William on 12 October 2016.

In LMS livery, No. 5407 passes the signal box at Mallaig as it runs round the train on 30 May 1984. The box was later demolished and replaced by a ground frame and a road has been built to the right of the line.

With the Small Isles as backdrop, Class 5 No. 44871 prepares to leave Mallaig station on 9 October 2004. The road behind the train was opened in 1988 on land partially reclaimed from the sea.

In the guise of No. 62012, the K1 waits in Mallaig station on 9 October 2004. The buildings behind the train were built on former railway land.